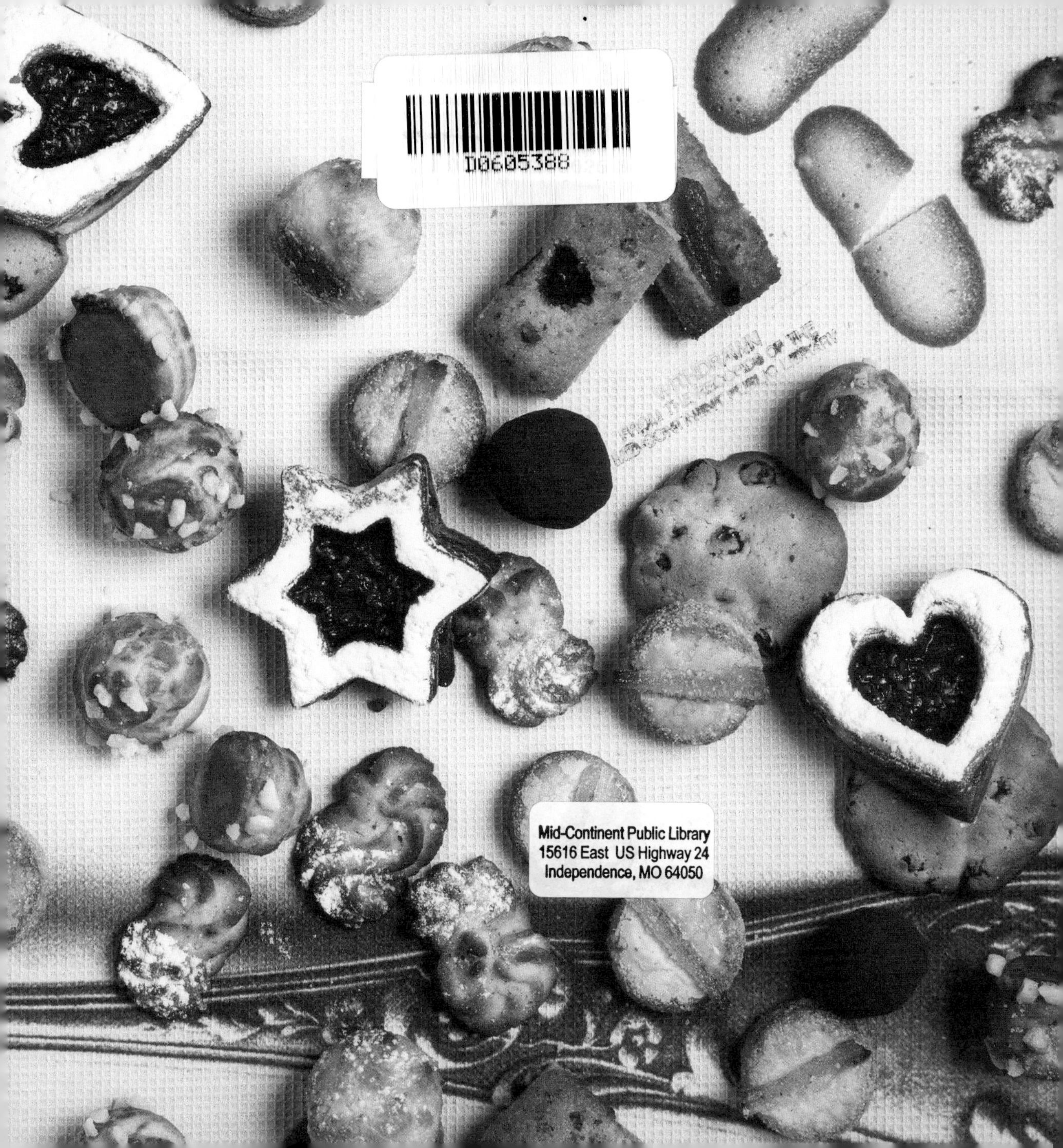

LES PETITS PLATS
FRANÇAIS
SIMON & SCHUSTER
ILLUSTRATED

coffee-time treats

JOSÉ MARÉCHAL

Photography by Akiko Ida
Styling by Camille Fourmont

SIMON &
SCHUSTER
ILLUSTRATED

London · New York · Sydney · Toronto
A CBS COMPANY

English language edition published in Great Britain by
Simon & Schuster UK Ltd, 2011
A CBS Company

Copyright © Marabout 2008

SIMON AND SCHUSTER
ILLUSTRATED BOOKS
Simon & Schuster UK
222 Gray's Inn Road
London WC1X 8HB
www.simonandschuster.co.uk

The right of José Maréchal to be identified as the Author of this Work has
been asserted by him in accordance with sections 77 and 78 of the Copyright,
Designs and Patents Act, 1988.

1 2 3 4 5 6 7 8 9 10

Translation: Prudence Ivey
Copy editor English language: Nicki Lampon

Colour reproduction by Dot Gradations Ltd, UK
Printed and bound in U.A.E.

ISBN 978-0-85720-251-2

Contents

Equipment

Cookie cutters

Round, square, with frilled edges, heart-shaped, star-shaped, in the shape of farm animals or letters of the alphabet… you can use any of these to cut out little biscuits.

Paper cases and silicone moulds

There are no particular instructions for using paper cases. They come in all sizes, can be white, brown or brightly coloured and you can find them in many shops. Watch out for metallic-coloured cases – gold or silver – they are more chic but traditionally, when used for chocolate, they have a tendency to stick!

You should be able to find many different shaped silicone moulds in specialist shops or online. They are not all the same quality and some are not heat resistant in very hot ovens. Therefore, be careful when cooking with them, especially when making Mini cannelés (page 44), which need oven temperatures of up to 240°C (fan oven 220°C), Gas Mark 9. You will need heat-resistant moulds for this.

Greaseproof paper and silicone sheets

I think that silicone sheets, which you can use without greasing, are ideal for all the petits fours recipes. However, if you do not have a silicone sheet, there are two alternatives: for cookies, meringues and biscuits that harden during cooking, line a baking tray with greaseproof paper to prevent them sticking; for things that come out of the oven a little softer and harden after a few minutes' cooling (such as tuiles or langues de chat) use a non-stick baking tray. Using a metal spatula, you can unstick these fine biscuits from a non-stick tray more easily than from greaseproof paper.

'Hot' milkshake

Preparation time: 10 minutes
Makes 4–5 milkshakes

4 scoops coffee ice cream
4 dessertspoons Baileys
4 dessertspoons milk
3 hot espressos

Put the ice cream, Baileys and milk in a blender or shaker.

Pour in the hot espressos then blend or shake for a few minutes.

Serve immediately.

Goes with... mini cakes (pages 48–58), Pertikus (page 62) and Langues de chat (page 68).

Hot chocolate

It's not just coffee that is delicious – a true hot chocolate recipe, simple and quick, works too! You can personalise this recipe according to the time of day and your mood. Add a little cinnamon, a few drops of kirsch or Cointreau or, even better, a big dollop of whipped cream for a gourmet hot chocolate!

Preparation time: 5 minutes
Cooking time: 8–10 minutes
Makes 4–6 drinks

1 litre (1 ¾ pints) whole milk
125 ml (4½ fl oz) water
100 g (3½ oz) caster sugar
200 g (7 oz) dark chocolate
   (minimum 70% cocoa solids)
30 g (1 oz) cocoa powder

Heat the milk, water and sugar over a low heat until boiling.

Away from the heat, add the chocolate and cocoa powder and mix well for around 2 minutes until smooth. Serve immediately.

Goes with... Chocolate cigarettes (page 24), Easy macaroons (page 46), Mini waffles (page 52), Mini brownies (page 58) or Double chocolate cookies (page 60) for an after school snack or a chocoholic brunch.

Irish coffee

Preparation time: 5 minutes
Makes 1 Irish coffee

30 ml (1 fl oz) whisky
20 ml (¾ fl oz) sugar cane syrup
1 hot espresso
50–80 ml (1 ¾–2¾ fl oz) whipped
  or very thick double cream

In a saucepan, gently heat the whisky and sugar syrup (be careful not to let it boil).

Once warm, pour the whisky syrup into a tall heatproof glass.

Immediately pour the espresso over the top. Lightly incline the glass or use a spoon to make sure the espresso forms a layer on the top and does not mix with the whisky. (Sugar makes the whisky denser, meaning that the lighter coffee can float on the top).

Add a layer of well-chilled whipped cream.

Drink immediately.

Goes with… Chocolate cigarettes (page 24), Chocolate tuiles (page 40), Pertikus (page 62), Ginger biscuits (page 64) or Langues de chat (page 68).

Coffee with spun sugar

This is a delicate and attractive way of serving coffee. The caramel filaments will sweeten and flavour the coffee and are sure to impress your guests. A little slight of hand is all that is needed. Since it is so fragile, the spun sugar should be prepared at the last moment.

Preparation time: 25 minutes
Cooking time: 8–10 minutes
Makes 4–6 coffees

80 ml (2¾ fl oz) water
250 g (8¾ oz) caster sugar
50 g (1¾ oz) glucose
4–6 cups hot espresso

Heat the water, sugar and glucose in a small saucepan and, stirring gently with a wooden spatula, bring to the boil.

Brush the sides of the saucepan with a damp pastry brush to get rid of any sugar crystals that start to stick to it.

Heat the sugar until it reaches 145°C (295°F).

Meanwhile, place a wooden spoon or spatula over a ramekin or small bowl on a smooth, lightly greased work surface.

Once the sugar reaches the right temperature, remove the saucepan from the heat and plunge the base into cold water for a few minutes to stop the sugar cooking. Leave for 3–4 minutes until the sugar cools slightly and becomes thicker.

Using two forks held tightly back to back, dip the spikes into the sugar then flick them back and forth over the handle of the spoon or spatula to create fine, long strands without lumps.

Remove the strands carefully and, without waiting, form them into balls in your hands (the same size as your coffee cups).

Serve the coffees with a ball of spun sugar resting on each.

Goes with… Florentines (page 14, for resting on the caramel) or Pertikus (page 62) and other biscuits (pages 60–71) for dunking.

Florentines

Your florentines will be even more special if, once they have cooled, you cover one side of them with melted chocolate. Florentines will keep for 8–10 days in an airtight container in a cool dry place (but not in the fridge).

Preparation time: 20 minutes + cooling
Cooking time: 15–20 minutes
Makes 30–40 Florentines

150 g (5¼ oz) double cream
40 g (1½ oz) butter
75 g (2½ oz) caster sugar
50 g (1¾ oz) honey
25 g (1 oz) glucose
100 g (3½ oz) almonds, sliced
50 g (1¾ oz) pistachios, roughly chopped
50 g (1¾ oz) candied orange peel, roughly chopped
50 g (1¾ oz) glacé cherries, roughly chopped

In a saucepan, heat the cream, butter, sugar, honey and glucose to 115°C (240°F). Away from the heat, add the nuts and fruits. Transfer the mixture to a mixing bowl and keep at room temperature.

Preheat the oven to 210°C (fan oven 190°C), Gas Mark 6½.

Make little balls of mixture and place in a silicone mould, on a silicone sheet (see Equipment on page 4) or on a non-stick baking tray.

Cook for 6–8 minutes. (Keep an eye on the florentines, they should turn golden but must not become too dark). You will need to cook the mixture in batches.

Leave to cool at room temperature in their moulds before turning out.

Goes with… truffles (pages 20–22) and biscuits (pages 60–71) for a mixture of textures.

Soft gingerbread meringues

Keep any collapsed meringues to serve with a creamy dessert or a fruit salad or to make layered desserts. These meringues will keep for 2–3 days in an airtight container, stored in a cool dry place (not the fridge).

Preparation time: 20–25 minutes
  + cooling
Cooking time: 20 minutes
Makes 40 meringues

275 g (9¾ oz) gingerbread
100 g (3½ oz) icing sugar
3 egg whites
50 g (1¾ oz) caster sugar

Preheat the oven to 180°C (fan oven 160°C), Gas Mark 4.

Cut the gingerbread into small pieces then mix with the icing sugar.

Cover a baking tray with a sheet of greaseproof paper, spread the sugar-coated pieces of gingerbread across it and cook for 6–7 minutes.

Meanwhile, beat the egg whites to form stiff peaks, add the caster sugar then beat again until firm. With a spatula, gently fold in the pieces of gingerbread.

Grease a baking tray and dust with flour. Pour the gingerbread meringue mixture on to the tray and smooth with a spatula until it is around 2 cm (¾ inch) thick.

Cook for 10–12 minutes, then leave to cool at room temperature for several minutes.

Use a cookie cutter to cut out the little meringues.

Goes with… Floating coffee (page 30) and Mini cream pots (page 32).

Nutty meringues

These meringues will keep for 8–10 days in an airtight container, stored in a cool dry place (not the fridge).

Preparation time: 20 minutes + cooling
Cooking time: 2½–3 hours
Makes 40 meringues

225 g (8 oz) walnuts
125 g (4½ oz) icing sugar
4 egg whites
175 g (6¼ oz) caster sugar

Preheat the oven to 180°C (fan oven 160°C), Gas Mark 4.

Mix the walnuts and icing sugar together.

Spread the nuts on a baking tray lined with greaseproof paper and put in the oven for around 8 minutes, stirring them after 4 minutes. Remove from the oven and roughly chop. Set aside. Reduce the oven temperature to 90°C (fan oven 70°C), Gas Mark ¼.

Whisk the egg whites until they have formed stiff peaks, add the caster sugar and whisk briefly until firm. Gently fold in the chopped walnuts.

Prepare a piping bag with a star-shaped nozzle and fill with the mixture. Squeeze the mixture on to a baking tray that has been greased and lightly dusted with flour. Cook for at least 2½ hours.

Leave the meringues to cool fully before removing them from the baking tray.

Goes with… Hot chocolate (page 8) – great for dunking!

White chocolate truffles

These will keep, covered in the sugar and potato starch mixture, for 4–6 days in an airtight container in the fridge.

Preparation time: 25 minutes +
  2½ hours chilling
Cooking time: 5 minutes
Makes 20–30 truffles

100 ml (3½ fl oz) single cream
220 g (7¾ oz) white chocolate,
  broken into small pieces
80 g (2¾ oz) unsalted butter, cut
  into cubes
20 ml (¾ fl oz) Cointreau or Grand
  Marnier
100 g (3½ oz) icing sugar
50 g (1¾ oz) potato starch

Heat the cream until it starts to simmer then, away from the heat, add the chocolate and butter. Mix well until you have a smooth ganache then add the Cointreau or Grand Marnier.

Put the ganache in the fridge for at least 2 hours until it hardens.

Mix the icing sugar and potato starch together on a large plate.

With a teaspoon, make little balls of ganache and roll them carefully in the sugar and potato starch mixture.

Arrange on a plate or in a plastic box and return to the fridge for 30 minutes before eating.

Goes with… Florentines (page 14), Coconut balls (page 36) or placed between two flat Orange tuiles (page 42) to create a mini millefeuille dessert.

Nutella truffles

The truffles will keep for 4–6 days if dusted with cocoa powder and stored in an airtight container in the fridge.

Preparation time: 35 minutes + 2½ hours chilling
Cooking time: 6 minutes
Makes 30–40 truffles

150 ml (5¼ fl oz) single cream
250 g (8¾ oz) dark chocolate, broken into pieces
125 g (4½ oz) butter, cut into cubes
200 g (7 oz) Nutella
200 g (7 oz) unsweetened cocoa powder

Heat the cream until it starts to simmer then, away from the heat, add the chocolate and the butter. Mix well until you have a smooth ganache then add the Nutella in two or three stages.

Put the ganache in the fridge for at least 2 hours until it hardens.

Put the cocoa powder on a plate.

With a teaspoon, make little balls of ganache and roll carefully in the cocoa powder.

Arrange on a plate or in a plastic box and return to the fridge for 30 minutes before eating.

Goes with… Florentines (page 14), Coconut balls (page 36) or placed between two flat Chocolate tuiles (page 40) to create a mini millefeuille dessert.

Chocolate cigarettes

Create the illusion of a lit cigarette with some gold or bronze cake decorating powder, carefully applied to the chocolate ends with a tweezer. These keep in the fridge for a maximum of 2–3 days. After that, the cigarettes will lose their crunch.

Preparation time: 20 minutes +
6–8 minutes chilling + setting
Makes 12 cigarettes

12 cigarettes russes
250 g (8¾ oz) icing sugar
2 egg whites
½ a lemon
80 g (2¾ oz) dark chocolate, broken
into pieces
a few drops of a neutral oil
(groundnut, sunflower, grapeseed)
gold or bronze cake decorating
powder

Chocolate ganache
150 ml (5¼ fl oz) single cream
250 g (8¾ oz) dark chocolate,
broken into pieces
125 g (4½ oz) butter, cut into cubes

To make the ganache, heat the cream until it starts to simmer then, away from the heat, add the chocolate and the butter. Mix well until you have a smooth ganache.

Using a piping bag with a narrow nozzle, fill the cigarettes with chocolate ganache. Keep in the fridge.

In a small bowl, mix the icing sugar, egg whites and a few drops of lemon juice. Mix vigorously with a spatula until you have a runny but thick royal icing (add 1 or 2 drops more of lemon juice if the mix is too thick, or a little more icing sugar if it is too runny).

Place the cigarettes on a cooling rack over a plate or baking tray and cover with royal icing, taking care to leave 1–2 cm (½–¾ inch) at the end to give the illusion of the filter. Place in a cool place to set (not the fridge).

Melt the chocolate with a few drops of oil in a bowl over a pan of simmering water or in the microwave. With a paper cone or a fork, drizzle the chocolate over the end of the cigarettes. Finish with a little gold or bronze cake decorating powder on the ends. Put in the fridge for 6–8 minutes until the chocolate hardens.

Goes with… Irish coffee (page 10) for total decadence or truffles (pages 20–23), Mini brownies (page 58) and Double chocolate cookies (page 60) for a chocolate feast.

Cherry coffee

Do not hesitate to vary this recipe by mixing different fruit (such as strawberries, physalis or grapes). The chocolate cherries will keep in the fridge for 2–3 days.

Preparation time: 35 minutes + 1½ hours chilling
Cooking time: 6 minutes
Makes 50–60 pieces

600 g (1lb 5 oz) cherries

Sugared cherries
125 g (4½ oz) caster sugar
50 g (1¾ oz) glucose
red food colouring (optional)
3 dessertspoons water

Chocolate cherries
250 g (8¾ oz) dark chocolate
2 dessertspoons oil

Cherry doughnuts
125 g (4½ oz) plain flour
1 egg
2 pinches of salt
1 dessertspoon oil
100 ml (3½ fl oz) beer
oil for deep frying
3 egg whites

For the sugar-covered cherries, put the sugar, glucose and food colouring in a small saucepan. Add the water and heat gently without stirring too much. As soon as the temperature reaches 118°C (244°F), remove the pan from the heat and put the base in cold water for around 1 minute to stop the syrup cooking further.

Dip a third of the cherries in the syrup, letting any excess drip into the saucepan, then place on a baking tray covered in greaseproof paper. Leave to harden open to the air. (Do not put in the fridge as the sugar will change colour in the humidity).

For the chocolate cherries, melt the chocolate with the oil in a bowl over a pan of simmering water. Dip each cherry in the melted chocolate, allow the excess chocolate to drip off, then lay on a baking tray. Leave to harden in the fridge.

To make the doughnuts, sieve the flour into a bowl and add the whole egg and salt. Add the oil and beer and mix all the ingredients until you have a smooth paste. Leave to rest at room temperature for a few minutes.

A few minutes before serving, heat the oil for frying over a medium heat. Whisk the egg whites until firm and gently add to the beer mixture. This will give you a slightly runny paste that is still thick enough to cover the cherries.

Dunk the cherries one by one in the batter and plunge them in the hot oil until they are golden. Drain off the excess oil with kitchen towel. Serve the cherries with coffee.

Coffee x 3

Preparation time: 30 minutes +
2–3 hours freezing
Cooking time: 5 minutes
Serves 4–6

4–6 espresso coffees

Coffee granita
200 ml (7 fl oz) water
100 g (3½ oz) caster sugar
400 ml (14 fl oz) strong coffee
a few drops of coffee extract

Mini tiramisu
4 egg yolks
60 g (2 oz) caster sugar
250 g (8¾ oz) mascarpone
300 ml (10½ oz) lukewarm coffee
3 dessertspoons amaretto
12 sponge fingers
3 dessertspoons cocoa powder

To make the granita, make a syrup by bringing the water and sugar to the boil. Away from the heat, add the coffee and coffee extract, then mix and leave to cool.

Put the syrup in the freezer and freeze for 2–3 hours, stirring every 30 minutes with a fork or whisk.

For a fine granita, you should mix for a final time just before serving.

For the tiramisu, beat the egg yolks and the sugar with a whisk until they reach an even, mousse-like consistency. Gradually add the mascarpone and beat vigorously.

In a bowl, mix the coffee and the amaretto and, one by one, lightly dip the sponge fingers in the mixture. Make a layer of soaked biscuits on the bottom of each serving glass.

Fill a piping bag with the mascarpone mixture and pipe a layer on top of the sponge fingers.

Make alternate layers of sponge fingers and mascarpone before finishing with a mascarpone layer.

Cover each tiramisu with cling film and put them in the fridge for at least an hour. Just before serving, dust with a layer of cocoa powder.

Make the espressos and divide the granita between matching glasses. Serve immediately.

Goes with… Chocolate cigarettes (page 24) and Chocolate tuiles (page 40), or serve Irish coffee (page 10) in place of the espressos.

Floating coffee

Preparation time: 25 minutes +
  1 hour cooling
Cooking time: 15 minutes
Serves 4–5

Coffee crème anglaise
250 ml (8¾ fl oz) milk
250 ml (8¾ fl oz) single cream
6 egg yolks
90 g (3 oz) caster sugar
1 dessertspoon coffee extract

Egg white islands
6 egg whites
75 g (2½ oz) caster sugar
a little oil, for greasing

Caramel
100 g (3½ oz) caster sugar
a little water

To make the crème anglaise, heat the milk and the cream over a medium heat until boiling.

Whisk the egg yolks and sugar until the mixture turns pale. Pour the hot cream over the egg yolks and whisk everything together well.

Return the custard to a low heat and stir constantly for 3–4 minutes. Watch out, the cream must not boil. The custard is ready when it has thickened and sticks to the back of a spoon. Add the coffee extract and stir in.

Leave to cool at room temperature for around 30 minutes then place in the fridge.

For the egg white islands, whisk the egg whites with 2 pinches of sugar. Once the whites have formed stiff peaks, add the rest of the sugar and whisk again until very smooth. Make small domes using a lightly oiled mould.

To cook the domes, either poach the egg whites in the crème anglaise for 2–3 minutes before removing it from the heat, or place the egg whites on a greased baking tray and cook at 80°C (fan oven 60°C), Gas Mark ¼ for 5–6 minutes.

To assemble the coffees, divide the crème anglaise between serving glasses and delicately place the egg white domes in the centre before making the caramel.

To make the caramel, heat the sugar and water over a medium heat, keeping an eye on it without stirring too much, until you have a pale caramel.

Once the caramel is a good colour, dunk the bottom of the saucepan in cold water for 1–2 minutes to stop the syrup cooking, then drizzle over the egg white domes.

Goes with… Soft gingerbread meringues (page 16), Chocolate tuiles (page 40), Mini madeleines (page 50) or Mini financiers (page 54).

Mini cream pots

These will keep for 4–5 days in the fridge covered with cling film.

Preparation time: 15–20 minutes
+ 4 hours chilling
Cooking time: 1 hour 15 minutes
Makes 25–30 mini pots

300 ml (10½ fl oz) whole milk
10 egg yolks
140 g (5 oz) caster sugar
900 ml (1½ pints) cold single cream

Flavourings
1 dessertspoon vanilla extract
1 dessertspoon coffee extract
1 dessertspoon cocoa powder
1 dessertspoon soluble or liquid
   chicory

Slowly bring the milk to the boil over a medium heat.

In a bowl, vigorously beat the egg yolks and the sugar then add the single cream. Add the boiling milk and mix well.

Divide the custard mix between four mixing bowls and add one of the four flavourings to each. (Dissolve the cocoa powder and the chicory powder in a little of the custard before incorporating it into the rest of the mixture).

Put the four creams in the fridge for at least 2 hours.

Fill little dessert pots with the custards and place in a roasting tin. Add boiling water to come halfway up the pots. Cook in a preheated oven at 90°C (fan oven 70°C), Gas Mark ¼ for around 1 hour 15 minutes. Make sure the oven temperature does not rise above 100°C (fan oven 80°C), Gas Mark ¼.

Once the pots are cooked, put them in the fridge for at least 2 hours before serving.

Goes with… Soft gingerbread meringues (page 16), Nutty meringues (page 18), tuiles (pages 40–43), Mini madeleines (page 50), Mini financiers (page 54) or Langues de chat (page 68).

Fast fancies

Gingerbread with orange
Cut a loaf of gingerbread into bite-size cubes, soak in freshly squeezed orange juice then ice with a layer of icing (icing sugar dissolved in a few drops of orange juice). Decorate with candied orange peel.

Mini marzipan chocolates
Take some marzipan that has been lightly flavoured with a liqueur or other flavouring. Cut it into pretty shapes with small cookie cutters and cover in melted dark, milk or white chocolate.

Rose and raspberry biscuits
Gently soak some Roses de Reims biscuits (available online) in a flavoured syrup and sandwich some lightly sweetened mascarpone and fresh raspberries between them.

Fun Mikados
Dunk Mikado sticks in different melted chocolates and decorate with chopped nuts to make these fail safe customised Mikados.

Chocolate cornflake nests
Melt some milk or dark chocolate with a little ground hazelnuts, stir in some cornflakes and leave to cool in small pieces on a baking tray lined with greaseproof paper.

Coconut balls

The coconut balls will keep for 4–5 days in an airtight container, in the fridge or in a cool dry place.

Preparation time: 5 minutes
Cooking time: 15 minutes
Makes 35–40 balls

250 g (8¾ oz) desiccated coconut
250 g (8¾ oz) icing sugar
5 egg whites

Preheat the oven to 200°C (fan oven 180°C), Gas Mark 6.

In a bowl, mix together the coconut, sugar and egg whites. Mix well until you have a smooth paste.

Roll small amounts of mixture in the palm of your hands until you have small balls of paste and carefully place them on a baking tray lined with greaseproof paper.

Cook for 12–15 minutes until the coconut balls are golden.

Goes with… Florentines (page 14) and truffles (pages 20–23).

Mini buns

Preparation time: 35 minutes + cooling
Cooking time: 35–40 minutes
Makes 60–75 buns

250 ml (8¾ fl oz) milk
250 ml (8¾ fl oz) water
200 g (7 oz) butter, cut into small cubes
1 dessertspoon caster sugar
3 pinches of salt
300 g (10½ oz) plain flour
7 eggs
150 g (5¼ oz) sugar crystals

In a saucepan, slowly heat the milk, water, butter, caster sugar and salt and bring to the boil, stirring constantly with a wooden spoon.

Remove the pan from the heat and immediately mix in the flour, mixing vigorously until it forms a smooth paste. Return to the heat and stir for a further 2–3 minutes.

Once the paste is shiny and dense, transfer to a mixing bowl.

Add the eggs one by one, mixing vigorously with each addition until you have a smooth, fluid paste.

Preheat the oven to 180°C (fan oven 160°C), Gas Mark 4.

Fill a piping bag with a small round nozzle with the mixture.

Pipe out small balls of paste, spaced 2–3 cm (¾–1¼ inches) apart on a non-stick baking tray. Using a fork and a little water, lightly moisten each ball and sprinkle with the sugar crystals.

Slide the tray into the middle of the oven, decrease the heat to 150°C (fan oven 130°C), Gas Mark 2 and cook the buns for around 15–20 minutes. Towards the end of the cooking time, open the oven door to gently lower the temperature.

Leave to cool before serving.

Goes with… Hot chocolate (page 8) or Mini cream pots (page 32) for an afternoon snack.

Chocolate tuiles

The paste will keep for 6–8 days in the fridge but the tuiles must be cooked at the last minute.

Preparation time: 20 minutes + 12 hours chilling
Cooking time: 12 minutes
Makes 30–40 tuiles

160 g (5½ oz) butter, at room temperature
240 g (8½ oz) icing sugar
80 g (2¾ oz) brown sugar
50 g (1¾ oz) cocoa powder
2 egg whites

In a bowl, mix the softened butter, both sugars and the cocoa powder until you have a creamy paste. Add the egg whites and mix again. Cover with cling film and put in the fridge for at least 12 hours.

Preheat the oven to 180°C (fan oven 160°C), Gas Mark 4.

With a teaspoon, scoop out hazelnut-sized balls of mixture and place them, well-spaced apart, on a non-stick baking tray. Cook for around 6–7 minutes. (You may need to cook them in two batches.)

Take the tuiles out of the oven and leave to cool on the baking tray for around 1 minute before unsticking them carefully with a spatula. To give them their classic curved shape you can bend them gently over a rolling pin while still warm.

Warning: The tuiles are very fine and fragile so be careful when handling them.

Goes with… make millefeuilles with flat tuiles layered with Nutella truffles (page 22) – they will make a great mini dessert.

Orange tuiles

These will keep for 4–5 days in an airtight container in a dry place.

Preparation time: 15 minutes +
30 minutes chilling
Cooking time: 15 minutes
Makes 20–30 tuiles

50 g (1¾ oz) butter
30 g (1 oz) plain flour
125 g (4½ oz) icing sugar
15 g (½ oz) ground almonds
grated zest and juice of 2 oranges
40 g (1½ oz) flaked almonds

In a small saucepan, melt the butter on a very low heat then take off the heat and set aside.

Mix the flour, sugar, ground almonds and orange zest together. Add 50 ml (1¾ fl oz) of orange juice and the melted butter and whisk. Add the flaked almonds and leave to rest in the fridge for around 30 minutes.

Preheat the oven to 200°C (fan oven 180°C), Gas Mark 6.

With a teaspoon, scoop out hazelnut-sized balls of mixture and place them, well-spaced apart, on a non-stick baking tray. Cook for around 7–8 minutes. (You may need to cook them in two batches.)

Take the tuiles out of the oven and leave to cool on the baking tray for around 1 minute before unsticking them carefully with a spatula. To give them their classic curved shape you can bend them gently over a rolling pin while still warm.

Goes with… make millefeuilles with flat tuiles layered with White chocolate truffles (page 20) – they will make a great mini dessert.

Mini cannelés

These will keep for 4–5 days in the fridge in an airtight container. Use silicone mini cannelés moulds (these will be cooked at a very high temperature so make sure the moulds are fully heat resistant).

Preparation time: 15 minutes +
  1 hour chilling
Cooking time: 1 hour
Makes 60 cannelés

500 ml (17½ fl oz) whole milk
60 g (2 oz) butter, cut into small
  pieces
2 eggs
2 egg yolks
250 g (8¾ oz) caster sugar
100 g (3½ oz) plain flour
a pinch of salt
1 dessertspoon rum
1 dessertspoon vanilla extract

Heat the milk and butter over a medium heat until the butter is melted.

In a bowl, beat the eggs, egg yolks and sugar until pale, then add the flour and salt. Mix well. Pour in the warm milk little by little, mixing with a whisk to get a fluid, lump-free batter. Leave to rest in the fridge for at least 1 hour then add the rum and the vanilla extract.

Preheat the oven to 240°C (fan oven 220°C), Gas Mark 9.

Fill a silicone mini cannelé mould two-thirds full with the batter (the cakes will rise while cooking and sink later on).

Cook for 6 minutes then reduce the temperature to 180°C (fan oven 160°C), Gas Mark 4 for 50 minutes to 1 hour.

Check on the cannelés: the outside should be dark brown but the inside should be nice and moist. Wait a few minutes before turning the cakes out.

Goes with… chic on their own, but very chic with truffles (pages 20–23).

Easy macaroons

The macaroon shells will keep for 2 days in an airtight container, but it is best to fill them at the last minute.

Preparation time: 15 minutes + cooling
Cooking time: 12 minutes
Makes 40 macaroons

125 g (4½ oz) ground almonds
125 g (4½ oz) icing sugar
4 egg whites
a few drops of vanilla extract

1 small pot of chocolate spread or 1 quantity of chocolate ganache (use the recipe for Nutella truffles on page 22)

Sieve the ground almonds and icing sugar together to get a fine mixture.

Whisk the egg whites until they form firm peaks, then fold in the almonds and sugar then the vanilla extract.

Preheat the oven to 210°C (fan oven 190°C), Gas Mark 6½.

Fill a piping bag and pipe small balls of mixture on to a baking tray lined with baking parchment. Cook for around 12 minutes.

Moisten a work surface before taking the macaroons out of the oven then slide the baking parchment on to it. This will allow you to unstick the macaroon shells more easily.

Stick the shells together in pairs with the chocolate spread or ganache.

Goes with… Coconut balls (page 36) and Jam biscuits (page 66).

Mini fruit cakes

The cake batter will keep for 3–4 days in the fridge. Once cooked, the cakes rapidly lose their moistness.

Preparation time: 30–35 minutes
 + 1 hour soaking + cooling
Cooking time: 15 minutes
Makes 30–40 cakes

80 g (2¾ oz) raisins
50 ml (1¾ oz) rum
250 g (8¾ oz) softened butter
250 g (8¾ oz) caster sugar
4 egg yolks
3 eggs
360 g (12¾ oz) plain flour
6 g (¼ oz) baking powder
150 g (5¼ oz) candied fruit

Soak the raisins in the rum for at least 1 hour.

Whisk the butter until it is very soft, then add the sugar. Beat again for around 2 minutes.

Add the egg yolks, then the whole eggs, one by one, mixing each time to be sure that the mixture does not curdle. Add the flour and baking powder and mix well with a wooden spoon. Add the candied fruit and the raisins.

Preheat the oven to 220°C (fan oven 200°C), Gas Mark 7.

If you are using metal mini cake moulds, line them with greaseproof paper to just over 4 cm (1½ inches) above the top of the mould (this is not necessary if using paper cases or silicone moulds). Divide the mixture between the moulds.

Cook for 6–7 minutes then reduce the oven temperature to 160°C (fan oven 140°C), Gas Mark 3, and cook for a further 7–8 minutes. Check the cakes are cooked through by pricking with a skewer: they are done if the skewer comes out clean.

Goes with… 'Hot' milkshake (page 6).

Mini madeleines

These keep for 2 days in an airtight container, although it is advisable to only cook them at the last minute as they are excellent fresh from the oven.

Preparation time: 15 minutes +
  1 hour chilling + cooling
Cooking time: 12 minutes
Makes 60 madeleines

125 g (4½ oz) butter, plus 40 g
  (1½ oz) for greasing
2 dessertspoons milk
3 eggs
200 g (7 oz) caster sugar
250 g (8¾ oz) plain flour
7 g (¼ oz) baking powder
grated zest of 1 orange
grated zest of 1 lemon

Melt the butter in a saucepan over a low heat, add the milk and set aside.

Beat the eggs with the sugar until the mixture turns pale.

Sieve the flour and baking powder together, add to the egg and sugar mixture and mix well. Add the butter and milk and orange and lemon zest. Mix well. Keep in the fridge for at least 1 hour.

Preheat the oven to 180°C (fan oven 160°C), Gas Mark 4.

Grease mini madeleine moulds with butter and fill them two-thirds full using a piping bag (the madeleines will puff up during cooking).

Cook for around 12 minutes. Check their colour. Turn the cakes out as soon as you remove them from the oven.

Goes with… Mini cream pots (page 32), Mini financiers (page 54), Raisin biscuits (page 70) and a cup of good Earl Grey tea.

Mini waffles

Make the batter in advance (it will keep well in the fridge for 24 hours) and cook the waffles just before serving. You will need a waffle iron for this recipe.

Preparation time: 10 minutes +
   1 hour chilling
Cooking time: 20 minutes
Makes 20–30 waffles

220 ml (8 fl oz) milk
220 g (7¾ oz) butter, cut into small
   pieces
110 g (4 oz) plain flour
2 egg whites
a pinch of salt
a little oil, for cooking

In a saucepan, gently heat the milk and butter until the butter is melted.

Put the flour into a mixing bowl and pour the warm milk into the flour little by little. Mix well until you have a smooth paste.

Whisk the egg whites and salt until they form stiff peaks. Gently fold into the flour mixture then chill in the fridge for at least 1 hour.

Heat a waffle iron and add 2 drops of oil to grease it. Make mini waffles using 1 dessertspoon of batter for each. Cook for 1–2 minutes each, re-greasing the iron between each waffle.

Goes with… melted chocolate, whipped cream and jam, 'Hot' milkshake (page 6) or Mini cream pots (page 32).

Mini financiers

These keep for 3–4 days in an airtight container in a cool dry location.

Preparation time: 25 minutes +
1 hour chilling + cooling
Cooking time: 6–7 minutes
Makes 60 financiers

150 g (5¼ oz) butter
130 g (4½ oz) ground almonds
225 g (8 oz) icing sugar
45 g (1½ oz) plain flour
8 egg whites

Flavourings
50 g (1¾ oz) desiccated coconut
50 g (1¾ oz) chopped pistachios
50 g (1¾ oz) raspberries
50 g (1¾ oz) dried apricots, sliced

Melt the butter in a pan and leave to brown slightly to get a slightly nutty taste. Set aside and leave to cool.

In a bowl, mix the ground almonds, sugar and flour together. Little by little add the egg whites and mix well until there are no lumps. Add the cooled butter and mix again.

Divide the batter between three bowls. Add the coconut to one, the pistachios to another and keep the third bowl plain. Keep in the fridge for at least 1 hour.

Preheat the oven to 210°C (fan oven 190°C), Gas Mark 6½.

With a piping bag, or using a spoon, fill mini financier moulds lined with paper cases (or use silicone moulds). Add a raspberry to the pistachio cakes and a slice of apricot to the coconut ones.

Cook for around 6–7 minutes. Leave the financiers to cool for a few minutes before turning them out.

Goes with… Floating coffee (page 30), Coconut balls (page 36) and Raisin biscuits (page 70).

Lemon mini muffins

These keep for 2–3 days in an airtight container in a cool, dry place.

Preparation time: 20 minutes +
 2 hours chilling + cooling
Cooking time: 10 minutes
Makes 60 muffins

100 g (3½ oz) butter, plus 50 g
 (1¾ oz) for greasing
250 g (8¾ oz) egg yolks
 (12–13 eggs)
380 g (13½ oz) caster sugar
260 g (9 oz) plain flour
6 g (¼ oz) baking powder
180 g (6¼ oz) crème fraîche
grated zest of 3 lemons

Melt the butter over a low heat or in the microwave.

Beat the egg yolks with the sugar until the mixture turns pale.

Add the flour and baking powder, mix well until there are no lumps, then add the melted butter, crème fraîche and lemon zest. Place the batter in the fridge for at least 2 hours.

Preheat the oven to 200°C (fan oven 180°C), Gas Mark 6.

Grease mini muffin moulds or line them with paper cases and two-thirds fill. Cook for around 8–10 minutes (depending on the size of the moulds).

Tip: If you wish, ice the muffins with icing sugar mixed with lemon juice.

Goes with… Orange tuiles (page 42) and Ginger biscuits (page 64) at teatime.

Mini brownies

Keep these for 5–6 days in the fridge, cutting into small pieces at the last minute.

Preparation time: 25 minutes + cooling
Cooking time: 25–30 minutes
Makes 40 brownies

220 g (7¾ oz) dark chocolate, broken into pieces
250 g (8¾ oz) butter, cut into pieces
3 eggs
300 g (10½ oz) caster sugar
110 g (4 oz) plain flour
40 g (1½ oz) cocoa powder
125 g (4½ oz) walnuts, roughly chopped

Melt the chocolate and butter in a bowl over a pan of simmering water or in the microwave.

Meanwhile, beat the eggs and sugar together. Add the chocolate and butter and mix well. Add the flour and cocoa powder. The mixture should be smooth and lump free. Mix in the chopped nuts.

Preheat the oven to 210°C (fan oven 190°C), Gas Mark 6½.

Pour the mixture into a greased rectangular tin.

Decrease the oven temperature to 180°C (fan oven 160°C), Gas Mark 4 and cook for around 25–30 minutes. The brownies should harden on the outside but remain soft in the centre.

Take out of the oven, turn out and leave to cool at room temperature. Just before serving, cut into bite-size squares.

Goes with… Nutty meringues (page 18) and White chocolate truffles (page 20).

Double chocolate cookies

Although these keep for 3–4 days in an airtight container in a dry place, they are best eaten on the day they are made.

Preparation time: 30–35 minutes
 + 2 hours chilling + cooling
Cooking time: 10 minutes
Makes 50–60 biscuits

250 g (8¾ oz) melted butter
150 g (5¼ oz) caster sugar
125 g (4½ oz) brown sugar
2 eggs
1 scant dessertspoon vanilla extract
4 pinches of salt
175 g (6¼ oz) dark chocolate chips
175 g (6¼ oz) white chocolate chips
325 g (11½ oz) plain flour
35 g (1¼ oz) cocoa powder
5 g (¼ oz) baking powder

Beat the butter and the two sugars together. Add the eggs, vanilla extract and salt. Mix well.

Add the chocolate chips then the flour, cocoa powder and baking powder. Mix until you have a smooth paste.

Make small logs of dough and wrap tightly in cling film. Place in the fridge for around 2 hours.

Remove the cling film and cut the logs into slices around 5 mm (¼ inch) thick.

Preheat the oven to 180–200°C (fan oven 160–180°C), Gas Mark 4–6. Place the discs of dough on a greased baking tray. Make sure they are well-spaced apart.

Cook for 7–9 minutes according to taste (cook for less time if you like cookies moist or longer if you prefer them more dry).

On taking them out of the oven, wait 2 minutes before removing the cookies from the tray with a metal spatula.

Goes with… truffles (pages 20–23), Chocolate cigarettes (page 24) and Raisin biscuits (page 70).

Pertikus

These will keep for 4–5 days in an airtight container in a dry place.

Preparation time: 15 minutes +
30 minutes chilling + cooling
Cooking time: 10 minutes
Makes 30–40 biscuits

170 g (6 oz) butter, at room
temperature
70 g (2½ oz) caster sugar
1 egg
200 g (7 oz) plain flour
85 g (3 oz) ground hazelnuts
a pinch of salt
2 pinches of cinnamon
2 drops of vanilla extract
grated zest of 1 lemon

Beat the butter and sugar together until they have a creamy consistency.

Add the egg, then the flour, hazelnuts and salt and mix well.

Add the cinnamon, vanilla extract and lemon zest. Put in the fridge to chill for 30 minutes.

Preheat the oven to 180°C (fan oven 160°C), Gas Mark 4.

Prepare a piping bag with a star nozzle and fill with the mixture.

On a lightly greased baking tray, pipe the dough into the shapes you want. Cook for around 10 minutes, depending on the size of the biscuits.

Goes with… Hot chocolate (page 8) and truffles (pages 20–23).

Ginger biscuits

These will keep for 4–6 days in an airtight container in a dry place.

Preparation time: 40 minutes +
1¼ hours chilling + cooling
Cooking time: 10–12 minutes
Makes 40 biscuits

250 g (8¾ oz) plain flour
150 g (5¼ oz) icing sugar
80 g (2¾ oz) ground almonds
1 teaspoon ground ginger
2 pinches of salt
4 egg yolks
150 g (5¼ oz) butter, at room
temperature, cut into small pieces
80 g (2¾ oz) caster sugar
1 egg, separated
80 g (2¾ oz) crystallized ginger,
sliced

Mix the flour, icing sugar, almonds, ginger and salt together. Pour the dry mixture on to a clean, dry work surface. Make a well in the centre and add the egg yolks and butter. Mix with your fingers, adding in the flour little by little until you have a paste.

Knead the paste, without pressing too hard, two or three times with the palm of your hand. Make a ball with the dough and put in the fridge for around 30 minutes.

Make small rolls of dough, around 3 cm (1¼ inches) in diameter. Roll them in the caster sugar, pressing lightly so that the sugar sticks well, then wrap in cling film and put in the freezer for 40 minutes.

Preheat the oven to 180°C (fan oven 160°C), Gas Mark 4.

Cut the rolls into 1 cm (½ inch) slices and put on a baking tray lined with baking parchment.

With a pastry brush, lightly coat the biscuits with egg white, place a slice of crystallized ginger in the centre and use beaten egg yolk to colour one half of the top of the biscuit. Cook for 10–12 minutes until the biscuits are golden.

Tip: You could also add lemon or orange zest to the dough.

Goes with… Orange tuiles (page 42) and Lemon mini muffins (page 56).

Jam biscuits

Have fun with these biscuits. Play with shapes and flavours to vary them and give interest to this recipe, which takes some time and precision but iss always impressive… Keep for 5–6 days in an airtight container in a cool, dry place. Fill at the last minute.

Preparation time: 20 minutes +
   30 minutes chilling + cooling
Cooking time: 15 minutes
Makes 12–15 biscuits

250 g (8¾ oz) plain flour, plus 100 g
   (3½ oz) for flouring
3 egg yolks
100 g (3½ oz) icing sugar
125 g (4½ oz) butter, at room
   temperature, cut into small cubes

Filling
250 g (8¾ oz) berry jam or jelly
100 g (3½ oz) icing sugar

Sieve the flour on to a clean, dry work surface. Make a well in the centre and add the egg yolks, sugar and butter. Mix with your fingertips, adding in the flour little by little until you have a paste.

Knead the paste, without pressing too hard, two or three times with the palm of your hand. Make a ball with the dough and put in the fridge for around 30 minutes.

Roll out the dough on a floured work surface until it is 5 mm (¼ inch) thick.

Using mini cookie cutters, cut out biscuit shapes and then cut out the centres of half of them with a smaller cutter. Carefully place on a baking tray and put in the fridge.

Preheat the oven to 180°C (fan oven 160°C), Gas Mark 4. Cook the biscuits for 15 minutes until they are golden. Leave to cool at room temperature.

With a spatula, spread the jam or jelly on the complete biscuits. Dust the biscuits with holes in with icing sugar.

Sandwich together the biscuits – jam on the bottom with the icing sugar on the top.

Goes with… Easy macaroons (page 46) and Mini waffles (page 52).

Langues de chat

These keep for 4–5 days in an airtight container, in a dry place.

Preparation time: 20 minutes +
 cooling
Cooking time: 15 minutes
Makes 40 biscuits

75 g (2½ oz) butter
85 g (3 oz) icing sugar
2 egg whites
60 g (2 oz) plain flour
½ teaspoon vanilla extract

Melt the butter in a pan over a low heat or in the microwave.

In a bowl, whisk the butter and icing sugar together. Little by little, add the egg whites, then the flour and vanilla extract.

Preheat the oven to 120–140°C (fan oven 100–120°C) Gas Mark ½–1.

Prepare a piping bag with a small round nozzle and fill with the biscuit mixture. Pipe small rectangles of dough, around 4 cm (1½ inches) long, on to a non-stick baking tray.

Cook for around 6 minutes until the biscuits are dark gold at the edges. (You may need to bake them in two batches.)

On taking them out of the oven, wait for 2 minutes, then unstick the biscuits with a metal spatula.

Goes with… Mini cream pots (page 32) or, used as an edible spoon, they will go with anything!

Raisin biscuits

These biscuits will keep for 4–5 days in an airtight container.

Preparation time: 10 minutes +
   1 hour chilling + cooling
Cooking time: 10–12 minutes
Makes 30–40 biscuits

125 g (4½ oz) raisins or currants
50 ml (1¾ fl oz) dark rum
125 g (4½ oz) butter, at room
   temperature
125 g (4½ oz) caster sugar
2 eggs
150 g (5¼ oz) plain flour, sifted

Soak the raisins or currants in the rum.

Beat the butter with the sugar until it turns creamy. Add the eggs, one by one, mixing vigorously after each one, then add the sieved flour to get a smooth paste.

Add the raisins and mix in. Place in the fridge for at least 1 hour.

Preheat the oven to 200°C (fan oven 180°C), Gas Mark 6.

Make small balls of the mixture and place on a well-greased baking tray, leaving plenty of space in between them.

Cook for 10–12 minutes: the biscuits should be golden.

Goes with… Nutty meringues (page 18), Mini financiers (page 54) and Double chocolate cookies (page 60).

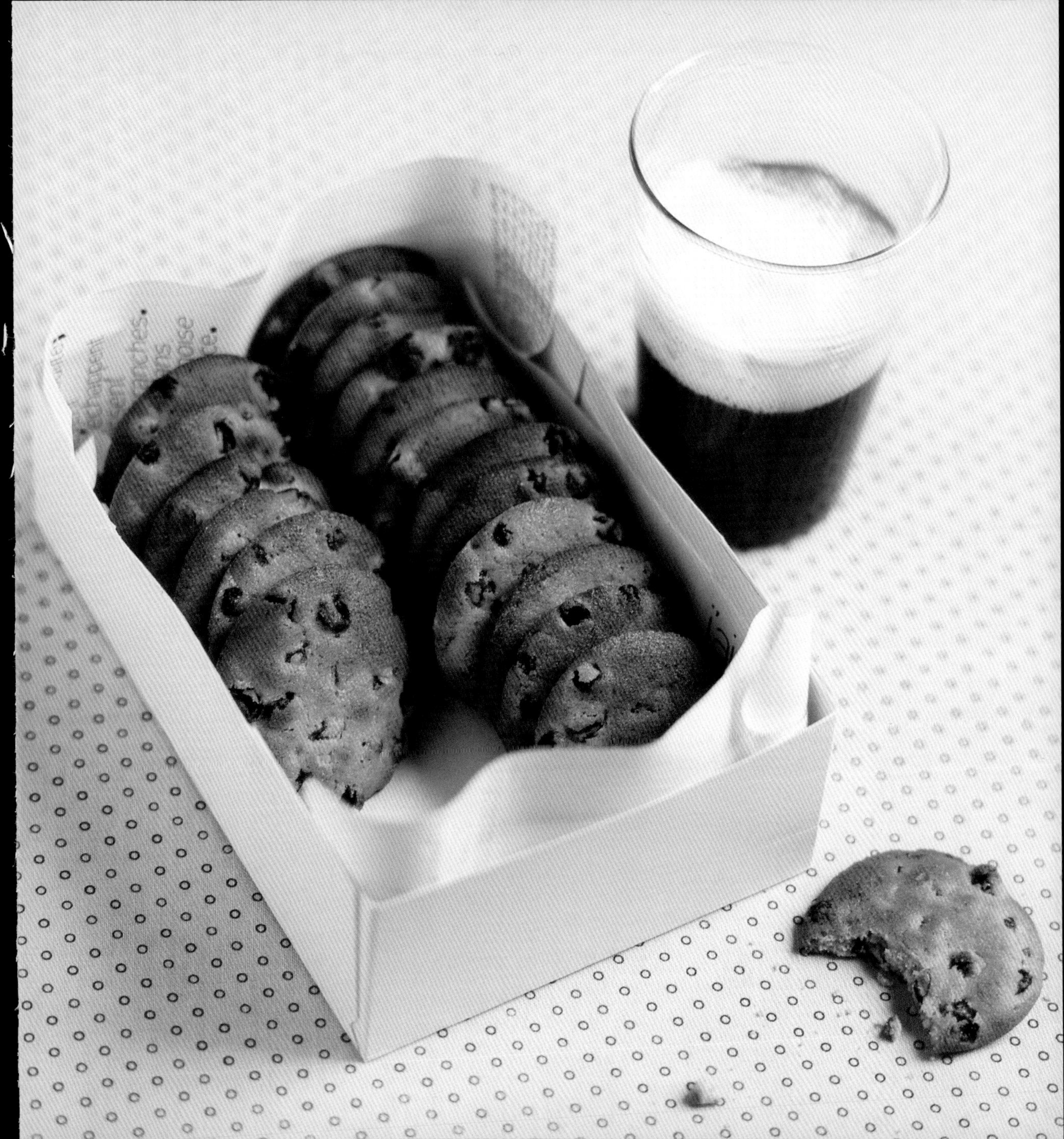

Index

Conversion tables

The tables below are only approximate and are meant to be used as a guide only.

Approximate American/ European conversions

	USA	Metric	Imperial
brown sugar	1 cup	170 g	6 oz
butter	1 stick	115 g	4 oz
butter/ margarine/ lard	1 cup	225 g	8 oz
caster and granulated sugar	2 level tablespoons	30 g	1 oz
caster and granulated sugar	1 cup	225 g	8 oz
currants	1 cup	140 g	5 oz
flour	1 cup	140 g	5 oz
golden syrup	1 cup	350 g	12 oz
ground almonds	1 cup	115 g	4 oz
sultanas/ raisins	1 cup	200 g	7 oz

Approximate American/ European conversions

American	European
1 teaspoon	1 teaspoon/ 5 ml
½ fl oz	1 tablespoon/ ½ fl oz/ 15 ml
¼ cup	4 tablespoons/ 2 fl oz/ 50 ml
½ cup plus 2 tablespoons	¼ pint/ 5 fl oz/ 150 ml
1¼ cups	½ pint/ 10 fl oz/ 300 ml
1 pint/ 16 fl oz	1 pint/ 20 fl oz/ 600 ml
2½ pints (5 cups)	1.2 litres/ 2 pints
10 pints	4.5 litres/ 8 pints

Liquid measures

Imperial	ml	fl oz
1 teaspoon	5	
2 tablespoons	30	
4 tablespoons	60	
¼ pint/ 1 gill	150	5
⅓ pint	200	7
½ pint	300	10
¾ pint	425	15
1 pint	600	20
1¾ pints	1000 (1 litre)	35

Oven temperatures

American	Celsius	Fahrenheit	Gas Mark
Cool	130	250	½
Very slow	140	275	1
Slow	150	300	2
Moderate	160	320	3
Moderate	180	350	4
Moderately hot	190	375	5
Fairly hot	200	400	6
Hot	220	425	7
Very hot	230	450	8
Extremely hot	240	475	9

Other useful measurements

Measurement	Metric	Imperial
1 American cup	225 ml	8 fl oz
1 egg, size 3	50 ml	2 fl oz
1 egg white	30 ml	1 fl oz
1 rounded tablespoon flour	30 g	1 oz
1 rounded tablespoon cornflour	30 g	1 oz
1 rounded tablespoon caster sugar	30 g	1 oz
2 level teaspoons gelatine	10 g	¼ oz

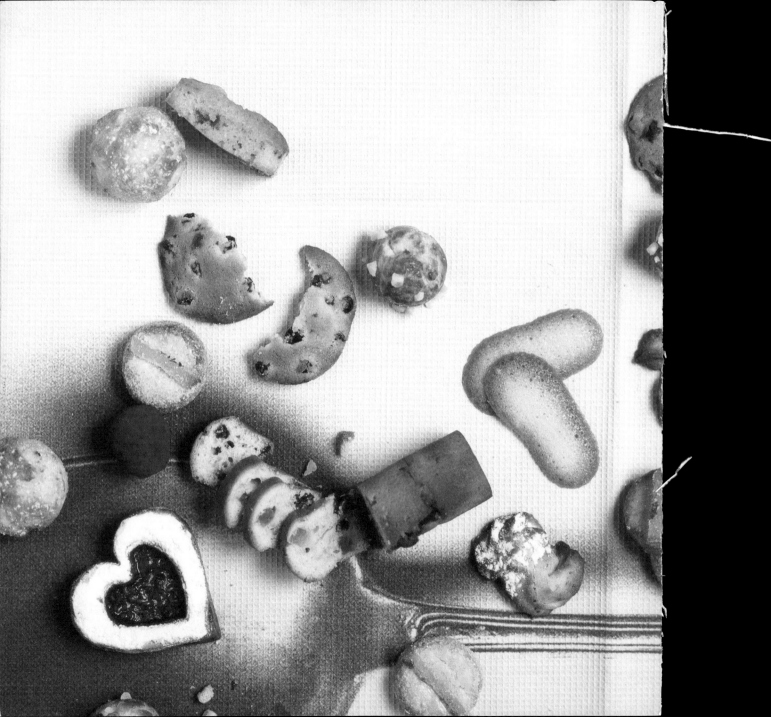